Too Little—Too Late?

Children's Evangelism Beyond Crisis

Penny Frank

Director, Youth and Children's Division, CPAS

Geoff Pearson

Vicar, St Bartholomew's, Roby, Liverpool Diocese

GROVE BOOKS LIMITED
RIDLEY HALL RD CAMBRIDGE CB3 9HU

Contents

The Cover Illustration is by Neil Pinchbeck

Church Army and the Grove Evangelism Series

Church Army has over 350 evangelists working in five areas of focus, at the cutting edge of evangelism in the UK. It co-sponsors the publication of the Grove Evangelism Series as part of its aim of stimulating discussion about evangelism strategies, and sharing its experience of front-line evangelism.

Further details about Church Army are available from:
Church Army, Independents Road, Blackheath, London SE3 9LG.
Telephone: 0181 318 1226. Fax: 0181 318 5258.
Registered charity number: 226226

First Impression February 1998
ISSN 1367-0840
ISBN 1 85174 366 9

1
Introduction

In 1991 it seemed that the church was in tune with the national mood. The Children Act had brought children into national focus. The Act emphasized protecting children, putting children first and giving them a voice in their future. It was followed by a painful national debate about the values we are passing on to our children, provoked by the abduction in Liverpool of a two year-old boy and his subsequent brutal murder by two ten year olds.

Internationally we have had some revealing insights into the destruction of childhood in Sarajevo through the diary of Zlata Filipovic.[1] Beginning her writing shortly before her eleventh birthday, we are taken into the world of a carefree girl increasingly circumscribed by the violence outside that keeps her trapped, often in the cellar. In 1990 the United Nations announced a Plan of Action intended to place children 'high and firmly on the agenda...giving them priority or "first call" on the world's resources in good times or bad, war or peace.' Many were encouraged to believe that a genuine social movement for children had begun to take shape.

Into this context Peter Snow on BBC2 *Newsnight* described the ecumenical report *All God's Children?*[2] and its statistic that only 15 children out of every 100 have any direct contact with a Christian church as 'reverberating around the ecclesiastical world.' Evidently the ecclesiastical world was not listening; the report is now out of print, and as the authors write it has produced too little, too late.

Engagement with children 'outside' church families is regarded as costly, unrewarding and controversial. Those who do it are often themselves on the edge of the churches they belong to, sometimes regarded as doing good work but not properly supported. It can be difficult to break out of a cycle which reinforces exclusion. Children themselves can be part of this cycle with children from church families not wanting 'their' church groups and activities taken over (or even shared) by outsiders.

When will we realize how far many of our children are from God? We are grieved to report failure but we are dealing with a whole generation without eternal hope, a generation that has not heard the Christian story about a heavenly father who loves them. Disaster awaits as the next generation of leaders are not being trained. We challenge you to read on and gain some passion for a lost generation.

1   Z Filipovic, *Zlata's Diary* (Viking, 1993) p 60.
2   *All God's Children?* (National Society/Church House Publishing, 1991).

2
Children Ignored

When the report *All God's Children?* was published, its back cover described it as a 'hard-hitting report which no church and no Christian can afford to ignore.' Now, as the report is out of print and no longer available to have that impact, it has to be accepted that many churches and most Christians have not even held it in their hands let alone considered the implications of its research or applied its message. In fact the church has slipped another seven years into the abyss, destined to be a body which chooses to ignore future generations of its members.

- Why did this report not have a greater impact in its day?
- The members of the working party were each deeply committed to its cause, so why were they apparently unable to produce a document for change?
- The situation in the church which had requested the report had worsened by the time the report was printed, so why was it not avidly read and implemented?

The subject of 'children' in or out of the church does not produce immediate interest and concern. Only when the news item is tragic or shocking does the average head turn to consider the situation. Those who are committed and involved with children already, either in a secular or a church setting, are usually finding it hard enough to survive with the level of work they already have; yet any more ideas and suggestions from the church usually automatically come to them. In society we hear the voice 'It's up to the parents' or 'The teachers ought to do something,' while in the church the congregation looks to its Sunday school teachers or the curate, all of whom are already fully employed. Those who were already concerned were already overwhelmed with their work with children, and those who were not concerned before the report remained unaware of it or unmoved by it.

The members of the working party each brought to the group different attitudes and philosophies about children and came from different theological and ecclesiastical persuasions. They worked hard to come to agreement without blunting the tool they were fashioning, but inevitably there were many issues where this was difficult—resulting in the rewriting of the report three times before it was acceptable to both the Boards of General Synod concerned. In the end perhaps the Boards were looking for something which was inoffensive.

However, in terms of the present state of evangelism among children we cannot but be offensive if we are being honest. The situation is appalling and the national church is in a state of almost complete lethargy as it is faced with a generation of children and young people who have not received their just inheritance:

1. Knowledge of the gospel of Jesus Christ.
2. Introduction to the character of God.
3. Familiarity with the teaching of Scripture.
4. Access to the wealth of Christian experience in the older generation.
5. Safe and appropriate opportunity for personal exploration and response.

Why did the report not break into this torpor and produce a reaction? Perhaps it was because of a shrinking diocesan commitment to children and young people—where any diocese is short of finance (as many are) the allocation for members of staff for the advising of work with the young disappears. Since money is where decisions are made and it is diocesan personnel who will have the impact in training and encouragement, many parishes have no heart to implement change—and in fact only half the parish churches in the UK are said to have provision for children now. Many dioceses have combined the posts of children and youth responsibilities, leaving one person to shoulder the expertise and the work of both, while others have joined the post to a half-time post of a parish priest—an insult to both the parish and a diocese full of children!

It seems we ignored these official recommendations of the Report:[3]

1. *'The Standing Committee of the General Synod should* report back to the Synod within twelve months on what arrangements have been made to ensure that the implications of this report have been followed through nationally within the Church of England and in partnership with other churches.'
    The Result? Waiting for funding now to set up a further working party.
2. *'The Boards of Education and Mission should* approach Churches Together in England with a view to sponsoring a conference of those responsible in the churches and voluntary agencies for the work of evangelism among children.'
    The Result? There has been no such conference, although in January 1996 a conference took place at the London Bible College called 'New Directions in Children's Ministry.' This attracted a large number of people already involved in work with children across the denominations. To some extent this led to networking about different projects and resources. The 'new directions' were not so obvious and many felt we covered old ground. The trouble is that it is hard not to cover old ground if the people do not already know each other well. One effect which the report did not have was that of

---

3 *All God's Children?* (National Society/Church House Publishing. 1991) p 89.

linking together people already involved in evangelism with children. Recently people like Viva Network and EA Network have started to make some sort of inventory of Children's Evangelists. If we are to make a difference and turn the tide for the children in the UK we need to work out a national strategy for achieving our aim. All those involved will then be able to see their area and role in the network. This could have happened as a result of the report but sadly did not.

3. *'Every Diocese should* identify a person to be responsible for encouraging and resourcing evangelism among children.'

The Result? Some have appointed an Evangelism Officer to reflect the Decade of Evangelism and may have included children specifically within that job description. This is unlikely in most cases. Evangelism among children requires specific skills not simply in educational terms and those of public communication but in understanding theology from a child's point of view being able to explain and illustrate it using a child's vocabulary. Expecting someone to transfer skills from adult to children's communication skills is asking a lot. In any case it is impossible in even the smallest diocese that one person could cover the demands of such a workload including envisioning, recruiting, training, resourcing teams of people as well as having time to show examples of good practice through exercising their own evangelistic ministry.

4. *'Every Parish should:*

a) '...assess its present work in the light of this report and take steps to ensure that the work has a high priority in its planning and resourcing.'

The Result? Very few have done so because those churches which have children's groups were already having such difficulty finding necessary leaders that it was impossible to consider catering for more children. Francis and Lankshear's report *In the Evangelical Way*, p 28, table 20 shows that while throughout the Church of England as a whole 65% of churches have contact with at least one six to nine year old on a typical Sunday, the proportion rises to 73% among the evangelical churches. Yet these churches struggle as hard as anyone else to find the leaders to resource their work—adults as a whole no longer want to spend their time preparing for a sharing group time with children.

b) '...encourage local Christians to support the work of Christian witness and the promotion of the spiritual development of pupils in schools by teachers, governors, parents and others.'

The Result? There is some evidence that this is happening. There are people who are responding to the challenge of the new responsibilities for school governors and churches who see that as the spiritual service of a church member. There are prayer groups for specific schools in some places. Teachers are under growing pressure and the number of parents who are involved in running Christian school clubs does not seem to have redressed the balance of the teachers who once were able to do so.

c) '...examine the demands it is making upon and the support it is giving to Christian parents including support for the Mothers' Union and other similar agencies.'

The Result? There is a growing concern to run parent support groups and many of these run courses for parents. Some groups have a particular emphasis for those who are leading a family on their own, or living within another culture, or implementing Christian principles. Some are run as first-stop evangelism to introduce parents from the community into the life of the church and to invite them to something like an *Alpha* or *Emmaus* course.

5. *'Every Christian should* seek ways of witnessing to his or her faith among families and children.

The Result? The result of this would be more people in church groups generally and certainly if we look at courses like *Alpha* we can see that there are encouraging signs. The people who constitute the *Alpha* statistics must include parents but at the moment there is no *Alpha* children's course. Some churches talk of growth in their All-Age Services which might point to families bringing families.

6. *'Everyone concerned with children should* ask what sort of church and society they would like to see in 30 years time—and what needs to be done now in order to enable that vision to be realized.'

The Result? Those concerned with children are overwhelmed by what they are already doing. Most of them are articulate about what their dreams and desires for the children are but they cannot do it on their own. Largely they are not the people who make decisions about budgets or who allocate people to projects—they are the people who do the work faithfully and often unthanked week after week throughout the year.

We also appear to have ignored the other recommendations within the Report:

- *Clergy Training.* 'It is well known that the colleges in our present system have a thankless task in trying to meet so many competing requirements and expectations. Nevertheless, it has to be reported that the picture which emerged from our inquiries revealed that no overall philosophy, little recognition of the significance of schools' work and very inadequate theoretical or practical provision...There is an understandable view of theological education which holds that initial training should concentrate on theology and spirituality to encourage the right sort of thinking, while practice is best learnt on the job...However, all too often, assistant curates find themselves thrown into the practicalities of their work from day one in the parish, therefore there is a need for an overview covering college and diocese to ensure that the right skills are taught at the right time' (page 63, para 6.11 and 6.12).

Such an overview has not come into existence within the years since the report was presented. Some colleges have changed their priorities so that children feature in the curriculum but most would say that the presence of the issue of children in a discussion depends on the individual voices of the students. This means that if a student is already interested in issues with children, the matter will be raised by the student and the whole group will benefit. If there is no such student the group will not be introduced to the topic. Ultimately it means that those who are already concerned will be the ones to continue their concern, whereas those who never think about children will not be stimulated to do so.

- *Leaders.* Those who are being encouraged to become involved in evangelism among children should be released from other responsibilities within the church (page 76, para 7.17). This is not happening in our churches. Often the people who are concerned about children in the community are the ones who already run activities for the children of church families. In many instances these are the parents of such children and frequently they are the ones whose energy is already being sapped not only by their home commitment but also by PCC, choir and church cleaning, and so on. We must encourage churches to set a high priority to children's evangelism so that the best and most appropriate people are freed to be involved.
- *The Spiritual Value of Evangelism.* The basic assumptions which the report says it is possible for us to make are these:
  1. We can assume that most children will respond to genuine love.
  2. We can assume that children are likely to show an openness to God.
  3. We can assume that our Lord is deeply concerned for children and that his Spirit is with us.
  4. We can assume that there is some profound meaning in the Lord's words that the kingdom belongs to children.
  5. We can assume that children can grasp the concept of Jesus as a 'special friend.'

In failing to respond to the recommendations of the report, we are ignoring the warning that the spiritual welfare of the children of our nation is at stake.

The short-term aim of evangelism of children is their enjoyment of God *now*. As they enter into that experience and knowledge they also often enter into the role of an evangelist themselves and invite their friends to the event which has helped them.

The medium-term aim of evangelism of children is that they will grow into leadership skills, gifts and roles in the church.

The long-term aim of evangelism is summed up by St Paul in Phil 1.6, that 'the good work begun in you should be brought to completion'—it is the same long term aim for children as it is for adults.

By ignoring the report and the desperate need for evangelism among our children, we are leaving children without the pleasure, joy and inner peace of knowing God for themselves now.. More than that, we are denying the church access to healthy and knowledgeable leadership not only now (children and young people have leadership gifts while they are young) but also in the future as they grow up into spiritually healthy adults. And we are ignoring the orthodox teaching of the church through the ages about eternal life.

If the gospel of Jesus Christ is true then by refusing to speak it out to our children we are allowing them to hurtle towards spiritual disaster without the concern which would put their well-being before other lesser matters.

3

Children at Risk

In 1996 *Signs of Life,* the Church of England's report for the mid-point of the Decade of Evangelism, was published. It commented 'The joint report of *All God's Children?* has been a major contribution to mission among children and young people. It has yet to be seen whether the Church will grasp the challenge represented by this report to put energies and resources into this area.'[4] The advocates on behalf of children still have a big task in hand. They can point to some progress but there are many hurdles in the way both old and new. A danger is always that the agenda will change quickly and children will be forgotten again. This threat has been very real with big agenda items such as the ordination of women to the presbyterate and the finances of the Church Commissioners. Advocates cannot assume that the momentum will automatically continue.

Child Protection and Child Abuse Guidelines

Another hurdle has been the necessary call from the bishops for child protection and child abuse guidelines. It is most important that the church and its leaders should have their integrity safe-guarded. Child abuse is a horrible reality and in some situations the reality is worse than fiction. The church in its pastoral care is concerned:

1. To protect children and vulnerable adults from the risk of abuse;
2. To equip clergy and others with pastoral oversight to know how to deal with

---

4   R Warren. *Signs of Life* (Church House Publishing) p 35.

a suspicion or complaint of abuse;

3. To protect clergy and others with pastoral oversight from the risk of being compromised or complaint of abuse.

Thus there is the need for the church to draw up guidance and good practice which can be agreed and then implemented by all involved. The danger is that some groups are in real danger of going too far the other way. In reaction it is possible to throw the baby out with the bath water by imposing rules that are too prescriptive, too strict and in danger of making people avoid work with children because the risks are too great. We do need guidelines but they need to be practical, realistic, safe boundaries. Contrary to popular opinion the Children Act does not really address the physical contact issue. Yet somehow the rumour has gone out that 'because of the Children Act, we are not allowed to touch children anymore.'[5]

Trying to keep the balance between under-reaction and over-reaction is very difficult. Polly Toynbee wrote an article in the *Independent* entitled 'The Age of Innocence is Dead, Killed by Suspicion—Child abuse fears are about to cost many needy children a holiday. Are we being over-cautious?'[6] The substance of the article is about the Children's Country Holiday Fund having to close down and stop 3,000 children going on holiday this year. Because of several incidents, and to avoid scandal, the charity, which has sent more than a million children on country holidays, has closed down. There is disappointment from the children, frustration from the volunteers who organize the holidays and the country families may feel themselves suddenly subject to unjust suspicion. Nothing groups can do will ever be 100% risk free. We do need good protective measures but if we over-react then the innocent will suffer and children's ministry will receive another setback.

Children Undervalued

In 1995 a working group of the Council of Churches for Britain and Ireland published *Unfinished Business: Children and the Churches.*[7] It argues that what children bring to the life of a Christian community is still undervalued and that nurture is still often limited to offering information about the faith rather than experience of it.

> 'In spite of all the words, reports and resolutions and of the prompting of many agencies, groups and individuals, the churches have not yet wholly been transformed into 'child-friendly' places either within their own life or as advocates for children in society' (page 1)

Unfinished Business continues the momentum of the children's agenda by encouraging us to act in the churches and in society alongside and on behalf of

5 S Green, *Children's Ministry* (March/April, 1996).
6 P Toynbee, *The Independent*, 1 May 1996.
7 Consultative Group on Ministry among Children, (CCBI Publications, 1995).

children. Some would argue that many have not started the business of having a much more positive role towards children. As yet we have not noticed any significant shift that has alerted churches to the seriousness of the situation regarding children. The response in the Church of England is patchy depending largely upon the commitment of each diocese to children's evangelism. Boards of Education tend, constitutionally, to be cool about evangelism and much prefer their earlier report *Children In the Way*[8] with its models for Christian education.

Family Breakdown and other Problems

Whilst in Britain today some children grow up surrounded by undreamed of material wealth, others have to cope with rejection and exclusion from the general improvements in standards of living in society (and within church congregations). In Knowsley, Merseyside, 40% of children are growing up in households where there is no working adult. This not only involves living on benefits but also the absence of a role model who is employed. Almost as many are living in families affected by adultery, separation, divorce and bereavement. Children have to cope with the loss of a stable family, often changing family composition, and the problems this causes.

In 1989 the Hillsborough tragedy involving the deaths of 93 football supporters hit Liverpool very hard. In the outpouring of grief it would have been easy to forget the children who also lost close family members. The Children's Society started work with young people affected by the tragedy and this developed into a project with children under-12 who have experienced traumatic events and bereavement. The project leader developed a practice model which created opportunities for the children to go out together, have a taste of adventure, have space to run and play, be together, use lots of energy, enjoy a picnic or meal and go home tired, often grubby at the end of the day. This was not just play; it was a means of adding positive experiences to the child's life to counterbalance the power of negative ones. Giving them positive 'normal' childhood activities to enjoy helped them to re-establish their self-confidence, to believe that the world is not all bad, to laugh and joke, to have a break from feeling gutted inside...they can eventually move on, not being stuck in their grief. Amanda Martin wrote about this in a private paper entitled *The Spiritual and Religious Dimensions of Resilience*.[9] She witnessed the restoring of a child's resilience through its own community of family, friends and neighbours. (This often involved a close relationship with an adult outside the immediate, often deeply grieving family.) Not surprisingly some of this experience has been shared with the community in Dunblane following their school tragedy.

---

8   *Children in the Way* (National Society/Church House Publishing, 1988).
9   A Martin, *The Spiritual and Religious Dimensions of Resilience* (Private paper, 1993).

'Rainbows for All God's Children'[10] is a scheme brought over from the States, designed to help children cope after death, divorce or separation, that has been taken up mainly by Roman Catholic Schools. Each group led by a facilitator meets for 13 weeks. The children use games, activities and stories, to work through their feelings under the following headings: self-feelings, death and divorce, angers and hurts, fears and worries, family, belonging, step-family, endings and beginnings, coping tools and reaching out. Although this worthwhile work continues with understandably little publicity, it is still only happening on a small scale compared to the tremendous needs all around, especially as the family ideal is under such pressure. The tragedy and challenge of so many damaged and hurt children still awaits a determined effort of energy and resources to turn the tide. There are so many needs amongst children and we are called not only to respond but also to offer new life in Christ. The following hymn is more than a cry about abortion. It becomes harder to sing the more we understand how many children are at risk in Britain today.

Who can sound the depths of sorrow in the Father heart of God,
for the children we've rejected, for the lives so deeply scarred?
And each light that we've extinguished has brought darkness to our land;
upon the nation, upon the nation have mercy Lord!

We have scorned the truth You gave us, we have bowed to other lords,
we have sacrificed the children on the altars of our gods.
O let truth again shine on us, let Your holy fear descend:
upon the nation, upon the nation have mercy Lord!

Who can stand before Your anger, who can face Your piercing eyes?
For You love the weak and helpless, and You hear the victims' cries.
Yes, You are a God of justice, and Your judgment surely comes:
upon the nation, upon the nation have mercy Lord!

Who will stand against the violence? Who will comfort those who mourn?
In the age of cruel rejection, who will build for love a home?
Come and shake us into action, come and melt our hearts of stone:
upon Your people, upon Your people, have mercy Lord!

Who can sound the depths of mercy in the Father heart of God?
For there is a Man of sorrows who for sinners shed His blood.
He can heal the wounds of nations, He can wash the guilty clean:
because of Jesus, because of Jesus, have mercy Lord!

(From Mission Praise No 766, Graham Kendrick 1988 Make Way Music)

---

10 'Rainbows for All God's Children,' c/o Dept for Christian Education, 152 Brownlow Hill, Liverpool L3 5RQ.

4
'Looking at Your Sleeping Face'

When BBC journalist Fergal Keane became a father he wrote a letter to his new son, Daniel Patrick, which the *Independent* published.[11]

'Your coming has turned me upside down and inside out. So much that seemed essential to me has, in the past few days, taken on a different colour. Like many foreign correspondents I know I have lived a life that on occasion has veered close to the edge—war zones, natural disasters, darkness in all its shapes and forms.

In a world of insecurity and ambition and ego it's easy to be drawn in, to take chances with our lives, to believe that what we do and what people say about it is reason enough to gamble with death. Now, looking at your sleeping face, inches away from me, listening to your occasional sigh and gurgle, I wonder how I could have ever thought glory and prizes and praise were sweeter than life.

And it's also true that I am pained, perhaps haunted is a better word, by the memory, suddenly so vivid now, of each suffering child I have come across on my journeys. Looking at you, the images come flooding back.

Ten year-old Ani Mikail dying from napalm burns on a hillside in Eritrea, how his voice cried out, growing ever more faint when the wind blew dust onto his wounds.

The two brothers, Domingo and Juste in Menongue, southern Angola. Juste, three years old and blind, dying from malnutrition, being carried on ten year old Domingo's back. And Domingo's words to me: "He was nice before, but now he has the hunger."

There is one last memory, of Rwanda, and the churchyard of the parish of Nyarabuye, where, in a ransacked classroom, I found a mother and her three young children huddled together where they had been beaten to death. The children had died holding onto their mother, that instinct we all learn from birth and in one way or another cling to until we die.

Daniel, these memories explain some of the fierce protectiveness I feel for you, the occasional moments of blind terror when I imagine anything happening to you.'

How can we get the church and society to 'look at a child's sleeping face,' to value children, to feel protective towards them, and to allow them to change

---

11 F Keane, *The Independent*, 9 April 1997, © Radio 4.

our lifestyle and our priorities? May we not lose the images of children who have been scarred by the world as we try our best to look after each little one that God brings to us in our family, our church, our Sunday School, or organization. In 1993 in *Save Our Children*[12] I pleaded for us to recognize a church stuck in an adult pattern of faith and the damaging effect such a church has on children's faith development. I still maintain that Christian maturity involves a Peter Pan-like, childlike attitude, a rediscovery of the child within. Becoming childlike is still the key to knowing the secret of faith (Mark 10.15).

New Models

In *Unfinished Business* one of the models or images of the church is that of the child.

> 'The Church as a child is dependent on God, receiving grace and blessings as a gift and living in trust...
> Like the child at play it is imaginative, inquisitive and spontaneous...
> It has no choice but to be powerless, to refuse the world's weapons, whether psychological, economic or military...
> It enjoys and celebrates life for its own sake rather than with some end or purpose in mind.'[13]

Another model of church in *Unfinished Business* is that of 'The Hospitable Place'— a place of hospitality and nurture offered with unconditional love, a place where children dependent, vulnerable and weak, can know that they can safely grow into 'the measure of the stature of the fullness of Christ' (Eph 4.13). It is to be a child-friendly place where children are made welcome and feel accepted, an open and accepting community where people are learning and growing together.

Both models cause us to stop and 'look at a child's sleeping face,' knowing that whoever receives one of these little ones receives Christ.

In history there have been turning moments when babies have been attacked—the births of Moses and Jesus for example. Some have suggested that the rise in abortions and what is happening to children world-wide may well herald the advent of the end times. We cannot sink into despair or wait for a supernatural deliverance. The gospel has the power to change situations. Researcher Patrick McDonald noted the particular power of the gospel in reaching street children, during a 15,000 mile, seventeen-city tour of projects through South America.

He was stunned to discover the 'obvious difference in success between the Christian and secular organizations...The results of the Christians were better

---

12 G Pearson, *Save Our Children* (Grove Evangelism Booklet 23).
13 *Unfinished Business* (CCBI Publications) p 61.

to such an extent that conclusions must be drawn...The difficulties of the lives of many of these kids requires answers very few people can give without the truth of the gospel.'[14]

Isaiah Vision

Nearer to home there is the challenge of the Isaiah Vision based on Isaiah 65.20–23.[15] This ecumenical strategy for congregation-based evangelism was developed by Raymond Fung when he was secretary for evangelism at the World Council of Churches. It is based on Isaiah's vision of the restored community in which both the young and the old find fulfilment and fill out their days, and people do not labour in vain but enjoy the work of their hands. In this strategy the local congregation, in partnership with other people, pursues the Isaiah agenda. The intention is to get involved with people, to work together for the concept of the Isaiah Agenda and in the process make sense of Christianity to those who are not interested in Jesus Christ. So in one local church all the efforts with after-schools clubs, holiday clubs, and partnership with residents association in employing part-time youth workers are part of the Isaiah Agenda. In the process of working towards the Isaiah Agenda the partners involved will grow to know and understand each other. Trust and friendship will develop. There will be opportunities to experience the Christian community and even further to challenge partners to follow Jesus Christ and to be members of the community of faith. The God we believe in is one who protects the children and does not want them to die physically and spiritually (Isaiah 65.20). This 'Agenda' can help us look afresh at the sleeping face of the child and hold us there long enough to see things in a truer perspective before God.

Weakness of the Pilgrim Model

On the negative side, one of the reasons for not looking at the sleeping face of the child is because we are too busy travelling alongside the child. Everywhere it seems the key concept is the journey and the pilgrim model. This journey of faith includes everyone, with some running ahead and some coming behind. Children are perhaps among those who explore ahead and alongside the path. The biblical image usually drawn on is the story of the Exodus and the wilderness experience of the people of Israel. There is a lot in this model and it links in with faith development and nurturing in the context of children's evangelism. Nevertheless there is a danger of forgetting that as well as sowing seed there are times of harvesting and reaping and this applies to children as well. We have become so used to the pilgrim model and the comfort of sowing seed that we have downgraded the work of the evangelist. We have too readily talked

---

14 P McDonald, *Street Kids in the Latin Americas* (Viva Foundation, 1993).
15 R Fung, *The Isaiah Vision* (WCC Publications, 1991).

about process and gradual conversions to the exclusion of genuine commitments which are more than children simply switching their affiliation. The 1945 report *Towards the Conversion of England* stated 'It is impossible to exaggerate the importance of bringing children to a simple and definite trust in God, by their acceptance of Christ Jesus as their saviour and friend.'[16]

It seems sometimes that we are happy to affirm children in the church and welcome all their contributions and yet we draw back at them becoming alive to Christ. We are so tuned often to the educational contexts in which we operate where we cannot make an appeal or encourage children to open the door to the knocking of someone without, that we have forgotten to do this in mission contexts. *Towards the Conversion of England* interestingly states:

'In the case of a definite call to decide for Christ, undue pressure and unwise emotion must be scrupulously avoided; but it should come to every child before the change from Primary to Secondary Education. It can be given through Sunday School lessons on Great Christians who made a definite decision for Christ or by a children's mission...In many cases there will be immediate results. In other cases a lasting impression is often made, so that a sudden conversion in later years can be traced to a remembered appeal in childhood' (page 88).

We are not seeking to impose adult models of conversion on children or to deny the many insights of faith development and development psychology but we may have gone too far in that direction. We are in danger of patronizing children by implying that they cannot really understand spiritual truths or make a meaningful commitment.

Children's Evangelists

We need more children's evangelists like R Hudson Pope who for fifty years led hundreds of boys and girls to Christ. He always used Bible words freely and told the children the Bible truths on which he was to act even if, at first, he could not understand them. He knew that the Spirit worked on the word and that time and the Spirit would explain. He expected decisions and he got them, all the way along. He expected and appealed to the child to come to Christ, to open his heart, to cross the bridge, to enter the door, to put his name in the envelope or to act on whatever metaphor he happened to have used. There is no method here other than being conscious of the guidance of the Holy Spirit. It meant that sometimes no appeal was made as he felt that it was not the moment to pull in the net. No high pressure or persuasive tactics were used. First and foremost was his constant communion with Christ and his complete dependence on the

---

16 *Towards the Conversion of England* (1945) p 87.

Holy Spirit. The practical outworking of this dependence might be condensed into eight factors:

1. He loved the children with a natural and a spiritual love.
2. He spoke with authority and simplicity.
3. He spoke of sin that they might be convicted.
4. He spoke of the cross that they might be saved.
5. He expected decisions—and got them.
6. He expected moral results—and saw them.
7. He taught them to be 'soul-winners.'
8. He committed them back to the care of their local churches, or followed them up himself.[17]

Early Harvest is a seminal book about leading a child to Christ by John Prince.[18] It is long out of print and probably considered out of touch with the contemporary religious education world. It deals with the general principles of spiritual counselling for conversion and then for the greater part how to apply those principles to the counselling of children. It is written on the experience of and the expectancy of children experiencing Christ in a valid way. Of course conversion is never an end in itself. There is still a life-long period of spiritual growth (or lack of it). But is has become too common in all the talk about journey and pilgrim models to minimize those crystallizing moments, especially the key one of spiritual birth.

Different Agenda

Yet another factor which stops us looking at the sleeping child is that there is so much else going on to catch our attention. People and organizations who might have a burden and vision for children have, it seems, burdens and visions for lots of other groupings. Two of the original working party of eight that produced *All God's Children?* have now become bishops and we know what multi-focus agendas they have to pursue. Organizations like Church Army and Church Pastoral Aid Society have targeted children as part of their future direction and put in lots of extra resources. However, they also have other areas of focus: Area Evangelism; Church Planting; Homeless People; Older People (Church Army). Just as we have Barnardo's and Children's Society which seek to have a holistic care for children we really need an organization that will have children's evangelism as a single focus. Dr Barnardo originally prepared for missionary service in China before founding his mission closer to home. On learning of the young doctor's change of plan, William Booth responded: 'You look after the children

---

17 P St John, *R Hudson Pope* (Scripture Union, 1967).
18 J Prince, *Early Harvest* (Falcon, 1976).

and I'll look after the adults. Then together we'll convert the world.'[19] The Barnardo's Home developed from this. Although there is still a need for such homes, for the safe homes run by the Children's Society, and for many organizations supporting projects among children, we still need a new focus to take forward a ministry of evangelism among children. Something like a newly formed 'Early Harvest' could focus on meeting the crisis of children's evangelism with particular attention given to seeking out and affirming children's evangelists. It could follow the example of King's Kids, who train children to develop their spirituality to witness and to exercise gifts of evangelism.

A Youth Conference in 1995 asked the question why the numbers of young people coming to church are decreasing. The young people felt strongly that if people of their age where to find church attractive it would have to regain its passion. Training, both relevant and up-to-date—'not just two weekends of training 20 years ago'—was essential for those whom local churches assigned to youth work. If there was both the passion and the training, then young people often dismissed as 'no-hopers' could instead be a 'Go generation' committed to extending God's kingdom 'out on the street, where the people are.' I believe the same applies for work with under 13s.

Face of God

Finally, as we look at the sleeping face of the children do we not also see the face of God? 'Whoever receives me receives not me but him who sent me.' To receive a child in the name of God is to receive God himself. God is represented in the child, for that he is like the child—God is child-like. How wrongly have theologians represented God. They have too often represented him as a great king on a grand throne wielding thunderbolts against those who take his name in vain and being over concerned about his glory. There Jesus is in the New Testament welcoming children and saying they are like God. The simplest parent who loves his children is a much truer type of our God than the kingly one. Childhood is part of the divine nature. The Lord has the heart of a child. Little wonder that Fergal Keane's baby turned him upside down and inside out. It happens again and again through the incarnation and through the love and witness of one who for ever shall be divinely childlike.

---

19 A Butcher, *Street Children* (Nelson Word Publishing. 1996) p 119.

5
Children Today

The report *All God's Children?* described the changes in society during the last 50 years and the situation in which we live today. Having done that, one of the processes which is then necessary is to look at the present situation and make deliberate conclusions about the way in which we need to alter our attitudes and approach to children in order to accommodate these changes. If we do not go through this process we will either simply leap to the conclusion that nothing will be successful because 'times have changed' or we will polarize our actions—going from one extreme to the exact opposite in our recognition that today is different. Both of these inappropriate reactions are obvious when we look in the church today for the attitude of the average person to children outside the church. The first attitude says 'Children are different now; they don't want to know; they won't come and even if they did they would only break the place up.' The second response is 'Children are different now; they are only interested in television and noise; they don't care about anybody except themselves; we don't have anything to offer them here.' If we look at a few examples of how 'times have changed' we will see that the way the church needs to respond and to approach unchurched children need not be defeatist.

1. Children Today are Fascinated by the Supernatural

Most popular television programmes today use a central figure with supernatural powers—invincible, laughingly sinister and triumphant at the end. Children in their own games often copy this supernatural model. What are the implications of this for evangelism? It probably means that instead of teaching Scripture as our first approach followed by an opportunity to experience God, we will need to be open to these happening the other way round. Many evangelists have found that unchurched children readily experience the presence of God and are ready to communicate by speaking and listening to God. The important role for the evangelist is to show by all that surrounds this experience that our only confidence and knowledge of this supernatural God is through the teaching of the Bible and in this way to grow the child's curiosity for what the Bible has to say about experience. In a non-book culture this needs to be done with imagination and creativity—*but* it does need to be done.

2. Children Today are Often Not the Top Priority in a Household.

Many children have one parent in their home and another in a separate household. This means that they are likely to be specifically spending time with one or the other at the weekends but often not closely cared for after school. The latchkey child is not from just the low-income families today and childminders, offering a safe place for them to do homework or play table games, are often in great demand. Here is the opportunity for the church—a safe place for fun, games and truth—to be that appropriate modern opportunity for evangelism. Yes of course the Children Act has made this more complicated but it has made it safer for us to do as well!

Secondly, because of this change in modern family priorities, children often live in an impoverished network of relationships. Some of them struggle to learn to trust people. To be with someone who has time to listen to them and to seek their opinion is a novelty. So a small club which gives committed leaders plenty of time to listen and chat informally is actually answering a modern need in a child. A home group situation with simple activities, story-telling and an opportunity to explore their opinions and experiences of God will be a popular delight to children. The trouble will often be to keep the group small because it will be so attractive to them.

3. Many Children Have Never Been Inside a Church

This can seem a problem if a leader is wanting to provide church-shaped answers. But local schools are often looking for a church to visit as part of the set work in the National Curriculum and many churches have realized that providing this can be an important first step in linking children in a local school with a church and helping them to feel more at home in the actual building—to take away some of the suspicion which is present in some communities between the churched and the unchurched. This needs to be done well—not simply leaving a key somewhere so that a class teacher can show their own class round but providing a stimulating simple tour of the building as a loving member of its community makes a big difference. The children may never be able to become members of the traditional church—there are people for whom the gap is simply too wide to cross in one lifetime. But they can find that Christians are safe people to listen to about God and that their homes are places where God is worshipped. A visit to the official building can be the start of this process.

4. Children in Many Cities are Confused by the Variety of Faiths

In this case, Christianity must be put in context when we talk about our faith. If they are having to make the comparison every time we talk about prayer or the Bible or the person of Jesus, why do we not help them to make that comparison? This will mean doing our homework about the faith groups which are in our city and really knowing what they believe and what their official approach to Christianity is. Many Christians simply ignore the presence of people of other faiths but children are usually at school side by side with other beliefs and it is unfair not to use a comparative approach to our evangelism and leave them to ask their questions to a non-Christian.

5. *Myths about Children Need to be Challenged*
a) Children are Sweet and Youths are Evil

It is amazing how attitudes grow. The fact is that there are pleasant children or teenagers and unpleasant children or teenagers just as there are pleasant adults and unpleasant adults. We need to get to know each other as individuals in order to find out. In the church we need to stand against an unreal impression of any age-group whether that is an idealistic one or doom and gloom. Leaders in our children's groups can often come off badly. On the one hand members of the congregation say that leading children must be thoroughly enjoyable if you have a calling for it—and completely ignore the hard work involved and the thanks which are due. On the other hand they are impervious to the need for more leaders, unaware that if they offered to become involved they would themselves benefit from the company and stimulus of children. We need to redress this and broadcast a real message about what children are like.

b) We Cannot Compete with Television or Local Sport

It is disheartening when there is a thriving timetable for children in your local area and not one obvious time when you can hold your club or activity. But the important first step is to do your parish audit. Find out what is already happening for children and look for the niche which is left empty and which you could fill. This needs to be done prayerfully and with imagination. You may benefit from some outside advice from a diocesan staff member or another organization. It is unwise to start simply by looking at the gifts and expertise of the people who have offered to be involved. If what you provide is not what your community needs then it is doomed to failure before you begin. An ideal starting place is to find the gap and pray for the right leaders, event or activity to fill it.

c) Parents will be Annoyed by Evangelism

In fact, this is rarely the case. If those involved are sensitively listening to children's questions and providing the opportunity to explore the answers, if they are offering activities at the time of day and week when families need support, there is rarely anything except thanks for an outreach club. Many parents of other faiths as well as those who hold to none will be enthusiastic in bringing their children or allowing them to come.

d) Teachers are the Main Source of Leadership

Today teachers are under more pressure and supported less positively by society than ever before. Many of them struggle day by day with unbelievable situations which only people of vocation would accept. It is unlikely that after a week in which they have struggled to survive, they would look at the weekend for the opportunity to be a leader of another group of children.

However, Christian teachers are concerned for children in and around the church. They are highly qualified and experienced people who have much to offer the church in terms of practical advice and creative suggestions. Instead of seeing them as a disappointment in terms of weekly leadership, why not invite them to become a consultant for other leaders. Many teachers welcome the opportunity to be involved in the training and encouragement of teachers once a term and leaders facing the opportunities with children every week feel more confident when asked to take on the role if they know that professional support is available.

e) Leadership is Exhausting

This is given as a reason for not accepting the position of children's leader or evangelist and it is a valid one. Many such people are poorly supported by the church and so it is inevitable that they will become dispirited and worn out. Those who take the evangelism of children and young people seriously quickly feel the effect of being in a spiritual battle. Their support and well-being must become of first importance to a church. If they are not seen to be well cared for, it is unlikely that others will want to join the team and those who are on the team will only be able to survive a short time. The programme of support for a full-time or volunteer children's leader involved in evangelism should include the personal and loving support of a small group who prays for them. It should involve opportunities to talk to the PCC and other leadership forums about the progress of their work. It must involve times when spiritual nurture is received by the leader. Too often the evangelism happens at a time when the rest of the church is receiving teaching, fellowship, communion and opportunity for sung worship. The leaders involved in evangelism will not survive long if they are regularly deprived of these basics.

f) 'I Need Professional Training to Work with Children'

People are understandably wary of taking on a responsibility for which they have had no training and little experience. In fact they will only be of short-term use unless they are trained to do the job. As soon as someone is invited to take on the responsibility and regular training and support are set in place, not only does the person feel valued and trusted—worth an investment—but the church can feel confident that the job will be done with increasing satisfaction and success. In some dioceses this training is not available because of the shortage of diocesan funds. In other dioceses there is a regular programme of training courses and consultation work. There are also organizations like CPAS which offer training and helpline consultation and parish audits. With the lack of training in children's evangelism available for ordinands in theological colleges, it is unfair to expect curates to train their team of volunteer leaders. They need the training and encouragement themselves.

6

Conclusion

The report *All God's Children?* has challenged churches to take children seriously. It still needs more energy and resources to be given for any serious effort to evangelize the children of this nation.

Children's evangelism, in the sense of offering children the message of good news and the opportunity to accept Christ and experience God's love, should be done within a setting where there will be continued contact and a chance to develop in faith and share in a Christian community. Most children who currently attend churches do so with at least one parent and it is usually parents of children who attend church who lead children's work. To reach outside this group of church families requires sustained involvement with children (and in due course adults) who are 'different.' It brings with it all the fears of working across cultures and is often only acceptable if 'they' are prepared to accept all 'our' ways of doing things.

As a starter we still need the conference recommended in the original report:

1) To raise awareness of children's work within churches across the denominations and encourage the churches both nationally and at a local level to increase their activity in this area.
2) To build up and disseminate a body of good practice in Christian children's work.
3) To set strategies for children's work in the future.

And Finally

The general public knew Dr Barnardo as a first rank philanthropist, the pioneer of children, the initiator of rescue work, the superb organizer, and the leader of British Youth into the broad spaces of the West. But deeper than all these great qualities (according to F B Meyer) was 'his faith in God and his walk with him.' Many owed more than food and clothing to Barnardo. William, for example, said at a crowded meeting of his mates and others. 'I owe everything to the Home, and I thank God I ever entered it. Mates, food and clothes are good things for a starving lad; but praise God, I've got what won't ever wear out, when clothes are in rags, and even if I am starving again. Now Christ is mine, and I am his; and when I think of His mercy in forgiving my many sins, and cleansing my wicked heart, I haven't words enough to thank him with, and feel I would like to spend my life in serving him.'[20]

---

20 Mrs Barnardo and James Marchant, *Memoirs of the Late Dr Barnardo* (Hodders, 1907).

Who today is carrying on that work of evangelism that Barnardo managed to combine so effectively with his other ministries? What chance would William have in the 1990s of hearing what God has done for him?